SCARECROW

March 22, 2016

SCARECROW

LEONTIA,

I'M SO GLAD TO HAVE
MET YOU, AND TO HAVE
HEARD YOU READ YOUR WORK.

~~Mark Callanan~~

ALL BEST,

killick press
an imprint of Creative Publishers

St. John's, Newfoundland and Labrador
2003

©2003, Mark Callanan

Le Conseil des Arts | The Canada Council
du Canada | for the Arts

We acknowledge the support of The Canada Council for the Arts for our
publishing program.

We acknowledge the financial support of the Government of Canada through the
Book Publishing Industry Development Program (BPIDP) for our publishing program.

Cover Photo: Manik Parab
(photo: Peter Pan statue at Bowring Park, St. John's, NL.)
Cover Design: Danielle Percy
∞ Printed on acid-free paper

Published by
KILLICK PRESS
an imprint of CREATIVE BOOK PUBLISHING
a division of Creative Printers and Publishers Limited
a Print Atlantic associated company
P.O. Box 8660, St. John's, Newfoundland and Labrador A1B 3T7

First Edition
Typeset in 11 point Perpetua

Printed in Canada by:
PRINT ATLANTIC

National Library of Canada Cataloguing in Publication

Callanan, Mark 1979-
        Scarecrow / Mark Callanan.

Poems.
ISBN 1-894294-68-8

        I. Title.

PS8555.A497S32 2003   C811'.6   C2003-904397-5

for my family
living and dead

and always
for Kate

CONTENTS

1

Chopping Wood

Leave all measure of this land behind
and the only distance
is implied by this slow stretch of birch,
the way their fingers
ache towards the sky

or cling desperately
to the wind as it flicks past,
reaching,
always, for something
to carry them
up into the night.

And the pain of separation is implied
by the rough smoke of burning bark,
loose curls of skin in the fire
that pop and crack flankers
out the open door
of the woodstove, fat with heat.

And if you follow me to the tree line
I'll show you
what you have known all along—
out here there is
only wood and cold.

I have burned everything
that could easily be named.

Farm

1

The smell of cow manure
steams the early morning
                    air.

A fight in the loft and the sting
           of a crab apple
           strikes your face

brings blood in great clots
to your nose.

There is nothing
so painful around here
and nothing

so exhilarating
           as the blood
           in thin rivulets on your lip.

2

To live life big,
an acre wide,
you have to take

one moment to stretch
yourself under the sun

and like a crab apple fallen
from its branch,

                  burn

in the midday heat,

your mind
a fury
of motion and fire,

your body
         rooted
in the tall grass.

Lying there.
Just lying.

Early Morning, Childhood

the stove-top kettle billows steam
coffee brews in the pot

my mother's hands work the dough
elastic pulled and squat

and everything centred
around her knuckles' thrust
down and through the counter

                until the open oven door

smell of bread
slowly rises with the sun

At the Butcher's Shop

Meat is meat and the block of wood,
two inches thick, is all that keeps
the knife from cleaving through the tabletop.
There's a pig on a hook by the window
that I swear has been eyeing me since I entered,
all two hundred pounds of him split open
and still nothing cut from the edge of his glare.
If it weren't for the hook he'd run off
madly squealing down the laneway,
past all the market stalls.

And the butcher's boy watches me as well,
his arms buried to the elbow in guts, apron soaked
with blood and his right eye dancing in its socket.
I ask for beef and edge uneasily away
from the pig as the butcher fills a bag, ties it up
and slaps the change into my palm
with an overhand chop.

There's something makes me wonder
as I'm walking out—
can the butcher, with all the blood on his hands
and his smock, his arms
crossed heavily against his chest,
resist the urge to see each passing animal
as two steps away from the chopping block?

After a Gelding

Jerking its head back in fits,
the neck muscles contorted, it twists
its legs upright—

> Samson stripped of potency,
> shorn locks ruffling
> on his pillow in the breeze
>
> and he, slack-jawed,
> staring at the scissors.

The horse rears up
and bolts off
down the meadow,

tramples flat
the tall pillars
of grass in his way.

The Delicate Touch Required for China

for Nan

My grandmother's hands were crippled,
twisted like roots sunk deep
into earth—

when she was young
they were two small birds
fluttering about their duties,

tying a shoelace,
bandaging a scraped knee

and, late at night,
taking my mother
by the hand
and leading her home over the dirt road.

I used to bring her tea
and watch her fumble with the cup,
balance it between two hands, wince
                at the delicate touch
                required for china.
The cracks in the cup
trailed off into her palms.

I remember her sitting on the edge of her bed,
fingers twisted useless around a brush.

> I used to sit behind her
> and pull comb through hair,
> stringing out her history in tangles,
> in waves thickly knotted.

> Her hair felt like rope
> in my small hands.

I remember her lying in a hospital bed,
still as stone,
seeing her dead at the funeral home,
her hands,
two clumps of earth.

In winter, my fingers ache with the cold.
> (the frost sinks deep
> into the cracks of my skin)

My hands are roots buried under mounds of snow.

Beach Stone

The stone is smooth
where the sea
has worn away its edges.

It rolls into the cup of my palm.

For all I know of rock,
it could be

the blunt tooth
of some long dead animal
fallen loose in decay,

or simply
a broken syllable

from the high sentence
of a cliff.

Without light
it is impossible to tell.

I close the stone
tight in my fist,

drop it into my front
coat pocket, just
as the last of the stars
wink out.

Snake

He wears the snake like an old wool scarf
as if the animal, eight foot
long and hissing like a pot boiling over
could not crush bone with its muscle—
the narrow head whipping, catches,
somewhere, the scent of meat.

Object Study

The edge of form blurs
into the scene— a stand of
trees becomes forest.

Running wolves, muscles
surging beneath the skin,
are reduced to pack, as if
this fury could be contained.

The snapping jaws,
saliva strung between
the teeth, the pale,
pale eye— as if all this
could be undone by diction.

A flock of gulls, each bird
a collection of bones
and sinew, hungry beaks
and bundles of feather and feet,

or the capelin all wet and slime
and scales running down
their backs as they surge
through beach foam, their tiny heads
probing pebbles under the sea.

Carpentry: A Poem in 5 Parts

1

One strike, two, the hammer
drives nails into boards.

2

My father's friend instructed:
measure twice before you cut.

3

I always trust my eye
as judge of angles, lengths.

4

I am a bad carpenter.
I rarely finish what I start.

One-Trick Pony

It's always the tango with him.
Request a mambo, break-dance,
two-step, salsa, foxtrot, flamenco,
jitterbug, waltz or ballet pirouette
and he's got four left feet,
his hooves ensnared in
their own wild meandering

beat.
       But boy can that horse ever
                    tango.

And when he holds you tight
to his oak-barrel chest, it seems
there is nothing left to keep you
both from a roll in the hay, his eyes
aflame. A suggestive toss
of his mane as he dips you
says the answer will be yes.

Made of Wood

things that are made of wood:

my desk, this pencil,
incense burner on the windowsill

picture frames, the bureau,
trees   (although I guess
                 that doesn't count)

the cross you gave me   (other miracles
                                 of carpentry)

coffins—   thick, heavy, oak

chests of drawers,
jewellery boxes   (your ring
                         inside)

my eyelids—
too heavy to hold
open, they close   (coffin doors
                         you inside)

me wanting to give
you one last chance
to crawl out.

Variations on a Theme

pain as pane
as window as glass
breaking as

painful as that sliver
that split the skin
beneath your lip as

painful as
kissing women
with shards of

lips the glass
stained in blood this is
painful but I'll try

to break it up for you
into neat shards maybe
into shattered

and the window
burst and

your heart is
glass and

this pain
will never break but

through the window
I'm watching
you undress

your lips
your skin

and everything is broken

The Man with the Twelve
O'clock Shadow

Doesn't shave much anymore, has cut himself too often
to keep his fingers steady on the blade; wears big hats that
shade out his eyes; is often broken in love, then scattered;
falls down when he walks, so watches carefully before
    he treads;
drinks a pint of whiskey a day for his health and carries
a six-pack of heat on his hip in case of trouble.
And he's always looking for that.

Trains don't run where he comes from
and the horses are all ship-ribbed with hunger.
There's a woman he left behind, of course,
with breasts as big as brass spittoons and
hair the colour of coins on a dead man's eyes.
But he never thinks of her anymore without reaching
for the straight razor, so he doesn't.

The sun, staring down on a scene with him
placed in a tavern, or on his back
in the middle of the red-dirt road, alone
can predict how long it is until he falls again.
No one else here knows his name.
The vultures, thick and liquid in the evening air,
are dreaming of his bones.

How to Bury Your Dead

1

With reckless abandon, at midnight, drunk
and ricocheting off gravestones as you slide
down the hill towards consecrated ground
with a body full of blood and water
that won't wait until morning
to put its soul to rest. The shovel, then,
becomes a weapon gouging at earth,
gutting the roots of trees that have bled
their way underground, lighting sparks
off rocks that lie between death
and the open graveyard air.

2

With solemnity, every move
a blessing and an exaltation,
touching your fingertips to your hat
in goodbye or god bless
and laying the body down
as slow as leading a child through water.

You guide the earth around the flesh
as if the ground is wanting,
as if you're plugging
a hole that aches
and aches to be filled.

3

With (and this is the easiest)
your eyes shut and the shovel
doing the dirty work,

emptying black earth
and filling it in again.

2

Lions and Lyres and Bears

Lupus

Trotting among the heavens,
his tongue lolling out,
pearl teeth glistening
and his hair, ragged
like an old winter coat.

His eyes are
twin harvest moons.

At the sight of him,
sheep and goat
turn tail and flee
and he bounds after,

tracks trailing
his paws' thrust— stars
printed in the night sky.

Canes Venatici

The pack. The growl.
The foaming mouth.
The beast as earth intended.
Bearing down on a rabbit,
they take their bearings
on the stench of the
meat, hot blood,
pulse and muscle.

Rabbit, in a frenzy, dives
down a hole. Deep
but never deep enough
and the hounds,
the hunting dogs
open up the ground,
clods of earth spitting
at the air, saliva
dripping from their jowls
until the rabbit, huddling
and calling the names
of all the gods he knows
is torn to pieces—

here a souvenir purse
and there a talisman
to ward off someone else's bad luck.
The dogs, smeared red with blood,
think on that irony
and laugh.

Ursa Major

The great bear and her son
down at the river, swatting at fish.

'You do it like this' she says, and swings
one paw towards the water,
tucking her entire body into that motion
so it comes compact—
one quick swipe and the fish,
Pisces, unfortunate son of the river
is thrown upon the bank to choke.

The little bear observes him
floundering, turns back
towards his reflection
on the water's face.

Capricornus

And then there's Capricornus,
the old goat, who, when
he's done running, is done
but for grazing over dead grass—
the bones of his jaw click
each time the teeth clamp down.

They say he'd eat anything
and considering the fact
that I've watched him consume

lead pencils, a fishing rod (hook intact),
a chrome fender, old tractor tires,
a black bowler hat, half
a Mercedes, the door off a barn
(the cows at least, were in shock),
the moon, earth, stars, a galaxy,
the universe

I'm not surprised.

Algol

The long   slow wink:
two stars passing each other,
changing positions,
but all you will think you see
is the one dimming down,
eyelid shutting in
the light of the face. All you'll see
is this wink, the sky watching
you, everything.

Taurus

He has gored
ten thousand matadors
and trampled the men
of Pamplona into dust,
their blood clotted in the earth.

But for all this
the arena holds him in.

The flowers,
oh the flowers that have been,
thrown at el matador
in his embroidered suit.

And once, Taurus,
ignoring all decorum,
threw himself into the air,
caught a rose between his teeth.

The ring of matador's
blood on his horns
would later come—

a wild rose bursting
into bloom.

Ara

Is the altar
where all
sacrifice is made

is the sweat
from the fire

      the heat and
      the anvil

is the pangs
in your belly
and your fear

      alone at night
      under the moon's
      razor

is loss
is agony
is despair

      bound up
      in chains and
      bleeding and weak

is the love
that is sacrificed
for revenge

is a burnt offering

is all that is left to you
when nothing is left

is more than
you will understand
until you've tasted
the rest.

Centaurus

Whose front legs are forever tangling
the one inside the other
and tripping
the steady rhythm of a trot.

Even the pastures are beginning
to resent it, the amateurish lope,
the inability to keep an even beat.

As he bears down on each
new fence, his human torso
hunched into the charge,

even the pickets cringe,
try their best to crouch.

Hydra

This one, many-headed and
slick as grease is
slipping through the water,
past a school of fish
and under the bow of the boat.
His back is all spines and
his mouth all knives and
he knows a meal when he sees one,
this one, and before
you know it he's charging
the surface and he's swallowed
the ship and you're sliding
down his dark throat— carried
on his way to devour
a belt of asteroids or two.

Lyra

When plucked, the strings produce
a harmony so sweet
as to induce the dead to rise and dance
above their tombs,
and tidal waves to crash and break
on far off coasts,
and fires to burst spontaneously in Rome—
the cityscape a ball of flame.

The music splits rocks
and parts oceans and empties rivers,
draws stars crashing to the earth,
shifts the beat of the heart in your chest
and injects your limbs
with fluid weightlessness—
and you dance as well.

None can hear the lyre but be broken,
in that instant, knowing
there is no turning back.

Corvus

Who, covered in pitch
by some delinquent youth,
is forever doomed
to squawk out his distaste
for flight as he cringes
on a fence post.

His vocabulary is far
too limited to express
the indignity of black.

Pyxis

It is the Mariner's Compass,
dead reckoning,
the only thing left
to lead you home
when the fog is so thick that
you can't see and you know
your heart is a broken instrument
that will not point the way.
There is only this contraption
in your hand, the constellation,
unseen above your head.

Carina

The keel of a boat.
But where is it going?

South? Towards that open patch of sea,
or north, toward the clouds
of flying fish that catch
the moonlight over and over as they leap

or right on down the river Styx,
the Panama Canal, the Straights of Gibraltar
or into St. John's harbour to stop
for a few quick drinks on the way to

> the Congo
> Nigeria
> Uzbekistan
> Malaysia
> Italy,

> with a drop
> kick down
> to Casablanca

and a brief stop in Nantucket
where all those quick syllables
lose significance in the dark
depths of a tumbler of Bourbon.

Oh   Carina, you
glorified batch of sticks,
I'll stay for the duration,
whatever tack you take.

Leo

Is the tough guy. Had a few
fights with a dragon
and a couple of scraps
with the sun over burning
far too bright for his liking.

He's pushed around
the odd wolf in his time
and feasts on every bloated
sheep he's come across.

He's got a scar over his left eye—
Orion beat him back with a club
A gouge in his right side—
the bull impaled, then lifted him up.

But for all that he's still standing.
And the sun's constant shining?

Hardly bothers him anymore.

Vulpecula

Who waits in ambush
for the odd chicken to cross
his path. He crouches
in a bed of twigs and leaves and
sniffs at the wind as if
tasting some unknown fare.
And deciding, perhaps,
that he's eaten better,
turns his tail and disappears.
The forest grows
around him as he runs.

Phoenix

And one final elegy
for the phoenix who,
knowing nothing else,
comes back, this time
his body burst against the grill
of a dark Sedan
and next, maybe sucked
into the turbine
of a passing overseas jet,
maybe on its way to Crete.

3

Notes towards a Greater Understanding of Flight

1

So obviously there's the bird
      with its wings extended
      like Christ himself on the cross

and I would explain the rest
but the currents escape me,
      so much hot air
      holding up
      starlings over the horizon

      like a trireme riding
      the crests and troughs of the Aegean.

I've been working on it for a while now,
      trying to pinpoint
      the exact moment when the earth
            begins
            to fall away,

      and sometimes the air around the wing
      takes shape, the pulse
      of muscle beneath the skin,
            and everything
            moves in waves.

But most times
        I've a mouthful of feathers,
        the cracked bones
of broken wings.

2

The falconer holds
                his right arm out
like St. Francis
to support the beast.
The claws clenching his forearm
pierce the leather glove.

Blinded by his hood, the falcon knows
somewhere in the sky

there is
a reason behind all this blue.

Wind ruffles his wings
as if to demonstrate
there is nothing left
on this earth to hold.

The hood is removed
and the day
           explodes

as the falcon
follows

the quick dagger of his beak
toward the clouds

to find
some answer in the sun.

3

The throttle snaps
forward and I'm pushed
back into my seat.

I'm thinking

      Newton, Newton,

third law or second?
Maybe the first.

      An object in motion
      tends to remain
      in motion.

      An object at rest
      tends to remain

but I can't rest in this plane.

The seatbelt pins
my hip bones down,
locks me in,

and the interior feels
like the ribcage
of some great beast— all steel
struts in place of bone.

A low rumbling from the flaps
turns my attention to the wings—
        metal plates
        an imitation of
        the feathers that began it all.

And outside this plane I'm sure
there's a starling I once saw
that's busy killing himself to catch up,
hurling his tiny frame
of feathers and hollow bones across the sky
because it's all he knows how to do.

I'm flying because
I want to forget everything else.

4

        An object in motion:

the starling, his wings
in perfect synchronization, up
and down beat.

And all the warmth
of the air cups his small body,
offers him up to the sun.

Magpies

The scrap-yard dog barks harmlessly,
jawing at a brood of magpies
high in the branches of an alder tree.

They're chatting over recent thefts
and this dog, born and bred
to detest the slightest whiff of larceny
is up on all fours resenting
the talk of their trade.

One says, "shit,
I wasn't four days hatched
before I snagged that diamond
necklace." "Zirconium,"
snorts another and the rest
titter at the joke.

Defeated by their high perch, the dog
drops down on his haunches,
weary face upturned toward the nest.

The youngest of the hatched,
eyes quick dark beads,
watches the metal collar
at his throat.

Conversation

With all this talk of Tufu
and everything,
I might have mistaken you
for the old poet
bent over the table,
leaning into me
almost shouting

I have seen such things

I bring to mind the story
of a sparrow you once saw
crushed in a bare fist.

You, leaning across the table,
almost shouting

my mind flying
past your stretching shoulder,
out the open door.

Song of the Crow

for Ted Hughes

escapes the dark throat—

no pretense of loveliness here,
like a dog it barks
note for note, the black

feathers

explode into flight,

the bird

glistens like wet pavement—

its throat, more bronze than silver,
its song plain

and beautiful like the empty
black womb of the sky.

Barn Swallows

But who owns it?
The barn I mean.
It's hard to say, but probably
an old man with a limp,
one eye to tell the time of day
and one to watch
the swallows in their flight,
their brief glide
down from the loft
to the hay-strewn floor.
Someone just like that.

The swallows sing
of blindness and other afflictions,
slit their own throats
on the stalks of wheat
then speed towards
their nests to sleep.
The swallows.
Who owns them? Probably
no one. Probably no
one but the wind.
Something as simple as that.

The Work, Work, Work of Art

Ode to Don McKay

Turn it on and crank it up
so the whole machine
shudders with delight
at the opening of valves
and turning of belts and
the pistons spitting flame.

Punch the dial past ten
and feel the gears grind
joyfully against each other,
rotation of hips and rotor cuffs
twisting in and out of place,

the whole contortion
of the thing, the beauty,
the sweet,
sweet hum of the engine,
perfume of gas and oil
boiling up and everything,
every
thing in motion,

all muscle and tendon and
pure joy to ride.

A Crow Drops

A crow breaks
from the foliage
of a nearby alder

drops
down over the field

one word caught
like a stone
in his throat.

He is black, a weapon—

arrow, sword,
hammer pounding

lightning
to the earth.

July Sketch

Two red-
throated sparrows

fly low over
the grass

wings spread
to cut
the shrill wind

until
they hit

some unseen
point
            and
ricochet
in opposite
directions

a low curve

their trajectories
set   for horizon

Talon

It's the feet that always get me,
walking in the tall grass in the garden
and finding the split bag of feathers
the cat left lying around.

The blood I can handle,
but the feet, broken twigs,
make my stomach surge
at my throat and I turn away.

The cat sits on the doorstep,
flicks his ears and waits
until I retreat inside
and grab a grocery bag,

my fingers rigid like a claw,
careful not to touch
the bone stiffness of the beak,
the thin rails of the legs—

the only remaining indications
that this piece of meat
used to sit on my clothesline singing

and, sometimes, spying a rustle
of movement in the bush,
rush to the air and escape.

Two For Joy

Two punk crows flapping
in the middle of the street.

One is the maniac
shrieking.

The other wheels
and struts around

a pack of garbage,
pokes at the black bags,

jabbing his head. The beak
comes up full of rotting bread.

Syllogism

with apologies to Robert Bringhurst

the sky is blue

the roofs in Japan are blue

      the sky is a roof

(can I patch it?)

clouds are the holes where tiles
have been picked off by wind

Throwing Voices

I can make it sound as if it comes
from most anywhere, around a
corner, from the top of the attic stairs
or the dirtied throat of a toilet bowl.

I can bounce it off a passing 747
and have it touch down in Kuala Lumpur,
Mexico City, or right plonk
in the middle of your backyard.

You'll hear me shout, 'hey you down there'
while you're trimming the hedges
or raking the leaves and think I'm god
or some crazed voice suggesting
murder in the kitchen
with the paring knife you use to cut the carrots.

But I'm not about any of that.
I'm a performer by nature, a sideshow act,
a touch of magic in the traffic of your day.

Listen. I can convince you you're hearing
an aria from a can of beans,
a joke told by a well-stocked freezer—
that foul-mouthed Christmas turkey
freezing his arse off in the corner.

Haiku

is not only form
it is the moment

> when one bird beats
> its wings and the wind

> learns the stiff curve
> of each feather

> and hungers
> for the next thrust
> of tight hard muscle.

when one man watches
a snowflake grow wild
and white and limber
and realizes

that crossing the street
today or tomorrow
won't matter

and that all the answers
he will ever need to know

are contained
in the sound

of a hailstone banging
off a tin roof—

      when a candle
      flame jerks
      against breath

      and the moment
      when all the lights
      are put out.

Scarecrow

A gull crucified
in a field.

The flies
circling his body

like the birds he wards off,

their wings buzzing
in the air.

And all that
bone, all that rot.

4

10 Journeys with the Moon as Guide

1

The moon mimics
my shiver on the
surface of the water.

Me, and the woman
I love, in the pond.

Or was there a third
that hid in darkness,
treading water

and swimming like that moonlight,
not sinking.

Not ever sinking.

2

The way I figure,
if I hold my eyes
open wide enough

I'll learn to decipher
one dark
shadow from the next—

the arm of the chair and
the curve of your breast
in perfect focus in this room.

I'll develop a new
form of sonar,

just whisper
into the darkness
and wait for an answer.

3

Places the moon has been:

over cafes in Barcelona,
over steamships on the Mississippi,
over battlefields in Carthage, in
the Belgian Congo, in
the South Pacific,

over children playing
spotlight
in backyards
in St. John's

over and over
and

over cornfields
glutted with crows

and over

junks sinking
off the coast of China

and over

knives falling
from the hands
of broken warriors

and over the plane that carried
my father back home

and later

over the pilot as he strode
to the apartment
of his mistress
with a ring in his pocket
and a song on his lips

and over
a sea of fir trees

and a school of capelin

and a lone hubcap shining
from the shoulder
of the Trans Canada

and over

your back
and your breasts
as you shed
your clothes and dove
into the water.

4

Simple logic

The moon pulls madly
on the tide.

The tide pulls at my
skin in the water.

My skin pulls me
about on a string:

       I am mad with
       the moon.

5

Now,
stare it in the eye.

Is it half full
or half empty?

Hard to say, isn't it?

Hard to see
through the clouds
on a night like this.

Use your imagination:
Is it
       the face of a quarter,
a canoe standing on end,
or maybe a bowl
to hold the night in?

Hard to say. Hard to see
what any of this has to do
with the way it snuck up on us
and laid its fingers on your skin.

Hard to say what this
has to do with anything, except

the moon has taught me
to think this way.

6

Errata

The moon pulls madly on the tide but
it was the undertow that pulled the flesh.
Skin is not responsible for the movement of the animal.

      The moon is mad.
      You are you.

7

It was the wolf that first got it right:
back on its haunches, mouth
curved to encompass the sky, to mimic
the moon's shape, to drink it in and exclaim

How bright! How bright!
This primitive god of night!

8

Among other things the moon is a crucial ingredient in ritual

the ritual of bathing in scented oil
of sweeping across a ballroom floor
of kneeling over toilet bowls
of filling a glass with wine
of reading by the fire
of sipping coffee on the porch

of dousing the last cigarette of the night
and of love, and all that

wonderful howling

9

Decipher
this dark
from another.

> You are the wolf
> she is the light

Just whisper
and wait
for an answer.

> I may never again
> see straight tonight

There was a third
swimming like moonlight
on the pond.

> I may never again
> see straight into the night

The moon is mad.
You are you.
Now.
Take a deep breath and

10

Howl.

Studies of the Island

a fresh cut
in the skin
of the Atlantic

salt and the smell
sometimes attached
to old wounds

bright blood
and copper, these
smells too

thin slips of grass
creeping up through
pavement

hot tar, old wood
the strict combination
of the two

the weight
of stones

their bold corners
rolling in your palm

rope and the method implied
(this I am only told)

the exact cut
of the wind

and the price
exacted on bare fingertips

any combination
of the above

vague gestures
the moon makes
behind clouds

all the prayers
balanced
on my tongue

the cold knit
of water
around your ankles

the breath
between
thoughts

the simple study:
rocks,
stillness

5

Lesson (1)

This wind is strong. It flares your hair
behind your head as you walk
with deliberate stride, elbows cocked
so your hands slide easily
into the pockets of your jeans.

You are ready for this, head
edged into the wind that rips
leaves from trees, topples
restaurant road signs, twists
your matted hair into furious motion.

You curl one finger around
a stray pen in your pocket and think
of all the words that have fallen
in between the minutes, the hours
and days that have passed.

It is raining now and the drops
are finding new ways to touch flesh,
strafing under the lips of umbrellas
to strike the face, soaking your hair
into fine points lancing out in all directions.

And all you can do is grip
down on the gust with your teeth
and keep moving, tough pavement
coming up to meet the soles of your shoes—

sharp rain teaching you
the exact shape of the wind.

Cabin

Take your bearings from the tree at the edge of your vision
and the woman watching from the cabin door
as you splinter birch wood to heat the oven
and warm your tiny room inside
where later you might talk or
make love, maybe and then, who knows,
sit up reading or fall asleep quick, entwined,
with nothing else in this life to do but hold.
The birch glows red in the stove nearby,
and her skin drifts under your fingertips, cool
and white like the smoke rising outside, that swims
through the loose net of branches and away.

Antique Shop

There's a terracotta cat
and a bone-carved
three-mast ship,
ebony candlesticks,
a china plate
and an urn, deep
blue and crafted from
something I don't
immediately recognise.

> It occurs to me
> on the bus
> as I'm riding home—
> it is the sea, the colour
> of the sea,
> and everything
> pours back into it.

Straight Razor

Through the window of the shop
you can watch
the old man working,

each flick of the razor
narrowly missing
an ear, the apple
at the young man's throat.

He's clipping hairs
as if there is no danger,
no potential for tragedy
on the barbershop floor.

I've often wondered
how one learns
to become fearless
with the knife.

Men have been killed
by blunter instruments, and this—

this razor is no dull artefact,
no cumbersome bronze
blade dug up from earth.

It is paper-thin, steel bright
with the glare of the sun

that watches, waiting
for each nick, each cut.

And love, also, is like this:
the sunlight off a razor
as it ducks and nips
its way around the flesh—

the beauty and
the danger of the instrument.

Silk Poem Number One

With what instrument can we measure
the whispers that silk makes in darkness?

The slight sound of your dress rustles
in this dark room—— words gathered,
filling the hands of the moon.

I give all I can offer: the strength
bound in muscle and the words
I have committed to memory.

Still, it is impossible to explain this night
and the dress you are wearing.

In darkness, whisper
is a word that rushes free of us.

My hands are empty.

Silk Poem Number Two

Whenas in silks
and all that stuff

and then a whisper
and then

nothing

no light
no sound   (and then?)

the thump
of your boots

dropping
to the hardwood

Things that Have Nothing to do with Fiji

Tell me how it rains in Fiji

or teach me something else,
something forgotten and old
like the back of your mother's hand

the worn parchment tracings
of her history— walking home at night
head tilted back, eyes wide
open to catch

a few words
slipping
off the moon's tongue

or the vague dizzying touch
of an infant steadying on your arm

and the moment
when each fibre of muscle
in his small legs begins
to read the new tilt of the earth's axis

quick jerk of his head
a new understanding of balance—

how swimming and bikes will follow
like the slow ache of rain from August sky

or teach me how
at the exact moment you stepped
from the train
the sun laid its rays
across the afternoon— the way
steel rails forge history across landscape

or teach me how a journey begins
with only

> a comb to impose some order on
> the tangles that have crept around your ears
> to whisper of wind and trees,

> and an amber stone because
> it is the closest thing you own
> to the shape of her breast

> and a sharp knife for rooting
> at the sole of your boot
> to make it loose enough to flop,
> catch dirt and rocks—

> sum total of this journey

how in leaving you learned
a lifetime of walking
the way home at night,

head tilted towards the sky
with the silver string
of a few words dangling
from between your teeth,

a few pebbles riding
in the soles of your boots

Japanese Bowl

Milan's writing poems about Japanese bowls again,
form and function married
in the curve of the lip,
the belly rounding out.

He examines how it cups rice,
or, turned upside down,
becomes a ridiculous helmet.

But as for creation?

Spinning on a potter's wheel,
the centre spreading to a globe,

smooth feel of the clay runs
the spaces between fingers.

Once baked in the kiln:

the bowl presses
tight to the open palms.

It's about context really.
I prefer the helmet.

Milan is dreaming of two
cupped hands reaching out
to receive.

Braiding Silver

I cannot fix
these broken things
only your braided ring—

four strands of silver
tangled as limbs
in the act of love,

my fingers probing
the surface of metal

seeking the groove
where one piece
would slide into another.

I worked for an hour
twisting the bands
over and over.

But these things exist
between us,

loops that coil
around my fingers
when I push,

that slip between spaces
and will not fit.

Wheelbarrow

for Allison

Roll on down this muddy road, the handles
guiding me like two prongs of a divining rod,
only on the slope, it's gravity that pulls
and not water. I'm carrying serious looking junks,
wood for the fire that will burn hotter
than hell, hopefully, or at the very least,
heat the living room through the winter's cold.

I've got a tuneless song on my lips and the whole
morbid weight of December on my mind, but I don't care.
I'm just rolling this wheelbarrow, catching some kind
of a rhythm as the wheel digs in and releases, digs
in and turns up earth, marking its lone tire track
along the path I travel— drawn by something stronger,
more urgent than the presence of buried water.

Divination

Like Cuvier reading the entire bird from the feather,
I'm learning to predict disaster in a drop of rain.
The entire predatory body of the storm will come later,
lightning inscribed on the parchment-ragged clouds.
From your kiss I read your leaving, my body
broken by whiskey and tears. But all of this came later.
Picture me now, a sort of modern-day Tiresias, stirring
   my fingers
in every pool I come across. I favour the rain collected
in dishes left outdoors for dogs. I favour dirty water.

Who favours me? The gods, occasionally, when they
   bless
the entrails of stray cats with visions of the future;
the rain, sometimes, which drowns out all the language
   in my ear,
that fills my mind with visions of the sea which seethes
   and
growls and sees nothing and hears nothing and never
   thinks
of the future. Let the ships and fish take care of
   themselves.
Let everything struggle to float above the wreckage and
   the waves.

Yesterday I happened to pass a birdbath and saw your
   face twinned.
What is the exact significance of the double?

Love appears in visions as a rose, failing that, the carcass
   of a horse.
Do you remember? You carved your name in my back
   with a finger.
But for the lightning forked in your eyes, I would have
   spoken it aloud.
Flower or carrion? (I can't remember)
I'm not the one in charge of metaphor.

It's no matter. Some day soon I'll find clean water,
sunk at the bottom of a well or falling clear to the foot
of a mountain, spilled as blood through the bone-thick
   rocks.
For now I'm off to strip each bird down to the feather,
piece my way from here back to the past we had
together. I'll burn it when I find it, as offering, as
   prayer.

Lesson (2)

We learn by going. There is no reading
up on this journey, no way of knowing
how the light will fall tomorrow on your face
and whether there will be rain or not.
And if the moon rises at your back as you walk,
then it rises, slow and in tune
with whatever stars have sung the night.

And if there's a woman you're leaving behind
with hair black as a crow, then there is
and she's waiting on the doorstep,
leaning up against the frame
with her arms crossed under her breasts
and maybe a few tears on her face.

And if there's an easier way of going
about this loss, then show me. If there's a path
leading down back alleys or through the thick of trees
to bring me, trudging all the way to the airport,
then lead me. I forget how to walk away from all this
and the scent of rose oil that clings to her skin.

In your absence, the morning sun will fall
on the crows and on her hair, but the rain will wash
you clean and the moon push you along the road.
It is only the wind that will speak her name.
Mind your step. The rosebushes on the path,
their thorns like fingers, will catch at your feet.

Last Word On Birch

Step off the plane at St. John's
and what happens next
is beyond you or me:

The birds hold their breath
and the wind, for a moment, ceases
to allow the pavement

room enough to halt its creaking
under tires and the rains to quit
their rushed conversation with the sidewalk.

Driving the way back into town,
you catch the scent
of birch burning in far off stoves,

the wisps of smoke plucked
from chimneys and dragged
across horizons by the wind.

The birds hold their breath.

It is beyond you or me. It is
beyond, even, the quick temper
of the axe or the stoicism of corded wood.

The horizon becomes a trail
of smoke leading eastward

to England, to God knows where,
to places I have never been

where silence is a word
and birch does not exist,
where nothing
is beyond anyone,
and the birds,

the birds are dark like smoke.

ACKNOWLEDGEMENTS

Some of these poems have previously appeared in the Canadian journals *TickleAce*, *The Newfoundland Quarterly*, *Lichen*, *Event*, *Grain*, *The Antigonish Review* and in the UK journal, *Poetry Life*. Section one of "Notes towards a Greater Understanding of Flight" was first published in *The Backyards of Heaven* (Scop Productions Inc, 2003), an anthology of Irish and Newfoundland writing. "The Delicate Touch Required for China" won first place in The Gregory J. Power Poetry Awards. "Things that Have Nothing to do with Fiji" and "Divination" both won Newfoundland and Labrador Arts and Letters Awards.

Thanks to Gordon for editing, Danielle for her work on the cover, Manik for the beautiful cover photo, my parents and my brother for their love and understanding, Milan, James, Steven, Bert, Mary D. and Mary B. for their various readings and critiques, encouragements, enlightenments and friendships, Anita for her voice and inspiration, the Best clan for the joy of their celebrations, Andrew, Oliver, Annette, Simon and the McCanns (big and small) for making a HOME for me in Yorkshire, Bill and Madge McCall for all those home-cooked dinners and conversations, The Packhorse and W.H. Smith Bookstore crowd for gathering me into the fold, Amanda (with apologies for slipping off), Karen for not killing me, Jordana who reminded me of many small beauties I'd forgotten along the way, Jen for her insufferable, inextinguishable flame and finally thanks to Kate for her love and patience, and beauty and passion.

MC